The Eye Witness

The Eye Witness

How Does Posttraumatic Stress Disorder Affect the
Intimate Relationships of Women of Color?

By

ANN PEAPIE

To order additional copies of this book, contact:
Xlibris
1-888-795-4274
www.Xlibris.com
Orders@Xlibris.com
702786

My Gratitude consist of thanking these individuals for their support

Lafayette Triplett Sr

Willie Mae Knox

Bennie Triplett

Clifford Hudson

Quincella Johnson

Charlene Edmond

Oprah Robertson

Evangeline Wright

Bernice McDonald

Connie White

Michelle Babbs

Ron and Faye Flemister

Table of Contents

Abstract

This book is about trauma, domestic violence, verbal, physical, and sexual abuse from the perspective of the eye witness. As a mental health clinician and a previous chronically mentally ill case manager in the field, I understand domestic violence and trauma dynamics. Apparently, I was not able to help myself from falling into the cycle of abuse. Fortunately, I reached out to my support system such as family and friends. This book focuses on traumatic events as reported by children, women, families, and soldiers. This book will also include stories mainly from females' perspectives while explaining the concept of Posttraumatic Stress Disorder.

Secondly, this book explains the definition of Posttraumatic Stress Disorder (PTSD) as found in the Diagnostic Statistical Manual IV and V (1994, 2013). Stories of African American Women and other ethnic background that have a diagnosis of Posttraumatic Stress Disorder and have experience traumatic event within the content of domestic violence are explored.

Their stories were chosen to address the question, "how does ethnic women cope with abusive issues within their relationships based upon on PTSD diagnosis." Also, examined are risk factors, legal and religious issues that might be involved when these women who have been traumatized by their partners.

In the spring of 1992 I was blown away by a tall dark handsome business man. This individual appeared to be a dependable and responsible person who loved God. He said all of the right things and did all of the right things. At that time I was going through an estranged relationship (ending my present relationship).

My previous spouse abandoned me after nine years of marriage. The oddest thing about this is how the relationship ended. In fact he vanished (disappeared) without any explanation. Several months later I heard from my spouse and he stated that he wanted a divorce. I quickly realized that he was serious. Most importantly he informed me that he wanted to go ahead with the divorce. Then he said I need to contact an attorney to file for a divorce without hesitating. However I followed his direction and filed for my divorce. At this point, I wondered if he was living a double life. Next, I learned that he was a part of a secret group and he was considered a defector.

Therefore he had to remain in hiding and not to be a part of society. After the divorced I felt depressed, alone, and guilty. The bottom line my self-esteem was very low. I also felt a strong sense of hopelessness and experienced suicidal thoughts. During this time one of my best friend spent a lot of time with me daily to keep me occupied. Next my aunt Vance prayed for my emotional and physical safety. I appreciated these individuals for their supporting me. I made it through the suicidal (Ideations) phase on one hand.

Although I found myself in an abusive relationship with a smooth talking business man (as I stated earlier in my introduction). This new relationship did not start out abusive. Initially, this relationship was romantic and passionate relationship. This kind of relationship appeared to be that kind of relationship that individuals dream of. I would say nothing is that good. This relationship was outstanding for several months. This man became controlling and obsessive out of the blue. After being in this marriage for about 10 months I experienced verbal, physical abuse, and sexual abuse (being raped constantly) by him. This relationship last for about 3 years, I attempted to leave several times but failed. I became afraid that he would have kill me. At times, I felt like I deserved the abuse and that he needed me. Now, I am living proof of the abusive cycle exists.

Finally I was able to leave him and things appeared to be ok. He was unaware of my whereabouts for a long period of time and how to find me. I did not know that he had been looking for me for several months. Evidently, he found me one day, tracked me down, followed me home, and broke in into my place. I could not persuade him to leave my place that night. He decided to stay overnight. I was so afraid that he would kill me throughout the night. So I went along with the verbal, physical, and sexual abuse. The next morning I explained to him that my supervisor expected me to show up for work that day. He allowed me to go to work.

Once I arrived at work my supervisor gave me some advised on how to get out of an abusive relationship. She encouraged me to submit a police report. I followed her direction and call my parents to come also.

Between filing the police report I decided to call him and inform him that I am not returning home. He became furious and destructive by cutting up all of my things and furniture. This was my turning point and I knew that I could not return back home. So my parents and siblings met me near my place. I approached my place and opened my front door and quickly glanced inside. I noticed that everything was destroyed (cut up). Then I understood that I had to get out of this relationship and moved to another state for my safety. This relationship was not shy of my spouse drug abuse, making fast money, and his aggressive life style.

In the summer of 1995 my family strongly encouraged me to move out of state. Once, I relocated to State of Washington I enrolled in the Women in Transition. This class taught me so much about how to appreciate myself and to make my own decisions in life. For the first time I understood what an abusive and emotional relationship is about. It appears that some men remain attract to successful women for various reasons. For example: they will not have to work as hard or they can throw away their money and do whatever they want to with their money. This class discussed subjects like the power of your decision in life and reinventing yourself. This class allowed me to gain control over my life in a positive way. I cannot not tell you why this happen to me during that time. Currently, I am aware of my past cultural surrounding included physical abuse, emotional abuse, and substance abuse as a child. My past frame of reference as it relates to what a healthy relationship looks like was not there. Therefore, subconsciously, I was attracted to what I seen as a child in my community about relationship. Most importantly what I went through cause me to seek to learn more about emotional abuse and domestic violence. My goals consist of learning how to avoid relationships that is controlling and abusive in nature. Next I will talk about emotional abuse and other types of abuse.

Emotional Abuse

I realized that emotional abuse is more damaging to one's character than physical abuse. Most importantly, both can destroy a person mentally, physically, and the professional character as well. For example, emotional abuse is constant and it appears to be never ending. This does not happen a few times but multiple times. Perhaps in forms of being nasty and ugly to the core. Emotional abuse is neither friendly nor supportive of the other person. Emotional abuse is about harassing, withholding affection and attention toward someone you claim that you care about. Next it include embarrassing the person in public setting, making negative gestures toward the person, and isolating them from social functioning, etc.

Unlike physical abuse, the people doing it and receiving it may not be aware of what is going on. It can be more harmful than physical abuse because it can undermine what we think about ourselves. It can cripple all we are meant to be as we allow something untrue to define us (Bogdanos, 2013). It is like you freeze emotionally and professionally.

Emotional abuse continues to occur among all ages, sex, religion, greed, and culture. Family and friends remains a product of emotional abuse at times. Generally, individual usually are abuse by someone they are close to or consider to love. Although the abuser may use negative words, display bad attitudes or promote their actions onto an unsuspecting victim. Especially when they have not dealt with their childhood wounds that are now causing them to harm others.

Unfortunately individuals who come from traditional or religious background may experience insults or domination of character. This may be due to the fact that the person may believe that they are superior and must maintain control over the victim.

For example, the abused person or the abuser may use statement or ask questions such as: (within these contexts below)

1. *Humiliation, degradation, discounting, is negating. judging, criticizing:*

o *They make fun of you and put you down for no apparent reason in front of your friends or coworkers*

o *They tease you and make condescending statements about you in hope of degrading you.*

o *They inform their friends and your friend that you are a "big joke" and never to take you seriously. Since they think you are stupid and may cry easily. (too emotional)*

o *They always tell you that you are wrong and that your opinion does not matter. (Just keep your mouth shut).*

o *They regularly ridicule, dismiss, and disregard your thoughts, suggestions, and feelings, etc.*

2. *Domination, control, and shame:*

o *They treat you like a child. (example: you feel like you must ask for permission to do everything)*

o *They constantly chastise you because of your inappropriate behavior based upon their perspective of you. (this destroy a person self-esteem)*

o *Not allow to spend money nor may any purchases for self. They purchases everything for you and tell you what to wear.*

o *They treat you as though you are inferior to them.*

o *They make you feel as though they are always right. (The victim feels powerless and begins to believe that their partner is right. Now the victim is gradually becoming a part of the cycle of abuse)*

o *Daily you are reminding of your shortcomings and that you do not measure up to the next person.*

o *They belittle your accomplishments, your aspirations, your dreams, and even who you are.*

o *They give disapproving, dismissive, contemptuous, or condescending looks, comments, and behavior.*

3. *Accusing and make unreasonable demands or expectations, denies own shortcomings:*

o *They accuse you of something they believe is true in their mind. You know all along that it is not true.*

o They cannot handle others making fun of them nor making any kind of comment that seems to show a lack of respect to them

o They make excuses for their behavior and mistakes. They may blame others for their faults.

o Yes, they will call you names

o They disrespect your requests and demonstrate repeated boundary violations. (the victim feels powerless and fearful)

4. Distancing, silent treatment, isolation, abandonment and neglect:

o They withhold their attention from you and isolate themselves from you.

o They fail to meet your basic needs and use this as a punishment

o They love playing mind games on you. Sometime they will deflect the blame onto you instead of taking responsibility for their actions

o They may choose to ignore you when you are speaking or seeking for help from them at times.

o *They fail to show empathy or practice unconditional regards for you. Neither is not interest in asking questions to help gather information for your benefit.*

5. *Codependence and enmeshment:*

   o *They treat you not as a separate person but instead as an extension of themselves.*

   o *They refuse to protect your personal boundaries and share information that you have not approved.*

   o *They disrespect your requests and do what they think is best for you.*

   o *They require continual contact and haven't developed a healthy support network among their own peers. The above statement about emotional abuse comes from the author perspective and from her resource database.*

During this time I had no clinical training about abuse, domestic violence, and Posttraumatic Stress Disorder.

Several years later this experience inspired me to go to college to understand trauma and abuse. I also decided to write this book based upon my family of origin history of abuse and my personal experience of being abuse prior to attending City University. After attending graduate school I learned that my father behavioral was abusive in nature. I do not know if it was related to his upbringing or things he witnessed during the Korean War. He was a Prisoner of War for several months (missing in action).

Eye Witness Testimonies (PTSD)

I would like to discuss two examples from the eyes of two soliders. These soldiers were bystanders and victims of war. They both experienced traumatic recurring dreams and flashback from serving their country. Once the SOLIDERS returned back to the United States and they were no longer the same. During those days they had little support in 50's and 60's for Posttraumatic stress disorder.

First, my father was drafted into the U.S. army in the 1950's. My father served in the United State Army during the Korean War. As a child, we observed my father experiencing flashback and being delusional. At an early age we thought dad was funny because he would have us marching around like little soldiers. We noticed that this happen every time he was sick or had a stroke or heart attack. This went on for many years the cold sweat and flashbacks. As a child it appeared that my father was in great distressed, reliving a Korean War event, having bout of angry spells, and fearful at the same time. During that time we had no clue that he was suffering from a mental illness. My father was missing in action across the enemy line for several months.

My grandmother convinced the Red Cross to find my father. He was found months later and shipped back to the United States. Once I graduated from undergraduate I learned from the local sheriff that my father was a military hero. He received this honor for saving so many souls lives during the Korean War. My father never talked to us about what he witnessed and experienced during the Korean War. However our county sheriff talked to us about how braved our father was and about things he had to do during wartime.

Second, a 58 year old retired solider heard about my 1st edition on Posttraumatic Stress Disorder from someone who attended one of my presentations on P.T.S.D. He went to through a lot to locate me. We finally scheduled a time to meet to discuss his concern. He brought a family member with him and they said that he had been trying to explain to his doctor his blackouts. During the meeting I noticed that he had difficulty staying track during our conversation. He frequently also lost track of time and he seem confused. It appeared that he would get frustrated often because he could not recall his last statement or sentence. I clarified with him this statement. Then I explained to him what was happening to him (Posttraumatic Stress Disorder symptoms). I also mentioned the types of support that he is entitled as a retired soldier. He felt relieved that he finally had some answers to his frustrations. From the information he gathers from our meeting he reported back to his physician. 30 days later I learned that he took my book to his military doctors to prove that he has been having flashbacks and blackouts. One he was able to clearly state his signs and symptoms the military approved him to received 100 disability.

The construct of Posttraumatic Stress Disorder was introduced initially in the third edition of Diagnostic and Statistical Manual of Mental Disorders American Psychiatric Association (1980) and revised in the DSM IV (1994). Kinchin (1998) indicates that the relationships of those suffering with PTSD from domestic violence will suffer in their daily activities. Adult women may struggle to maintain a satisfactory partnership, be a poor parent, wrestle with their career and play a lesser part in their community life than they would originally have wished. Many victims allow feelings of guilt and shame to dominate their lives.

This research book will initially examine the DSM IV criteria of Posttraumatic Stress Disorder and trauma. Journal articles and books will then be critically reviewed on the issues of Posttraumatic Stress Disorder and trauma. Finally, focus will turn to how women cope with Posttraumatic Stress Disorder in their intimate

relationships.

Definitions

<u>Posttraumatic Stress Disorder</u>

Posttraumatic stress disorders are a natural emotional

reaction to a deeply shocking and disturbing experience.

It is a normal reaction to an abnormal situation. The more

severe the trauma, the longer these symptoms will persist.

In cases of major and or repeated trauma, strong reactions

may continue for years (DSM IV, 1994). A traumatic event

resulting in a diagnosis of PTSD can cause changes in your

brain chemistry. These changes are helpful in the short term

because they reduce the level of emotions to something

bearable. They are harmful in the long term because they

reinforce and maintain the PTSD symptoms.

As a current survivor of Posttraumatic Stress Disorder

I concur with the definition of P.T.S.D. In the mid 80's I

experienced being severely abuse physically and emotionally.

This was one of the most confusing times of my life. At first

I did not have a clue that I was being affect to the point of feeling lose and being paralyze in my mind. Most of the time I felt like a child and felt lost somewhere in middle of nowhere. I could not recall having information, had problem memorizing things, and trying to think of simple thing. When I read articles from magazines or the newspapers I barely recall half of one sentence.

The DSM - 5 criteria is similar to DSM IV definition of Posttraumatic Stress Disorder. Even though the DSM-5 underwent significant changes. For Instance the diagnosis of "Sexual assault is recurring exposure that could apply to police officers or first responders. This language below has been removed from the DSM IV manual which states individual reaction to the event may consist of intense fear, helplessness or horror.

In addition the clusters for PTSD symptoms based upon the DSM-5 (2013) updates has included several **clusters:**

- *Re - living the event such as having memories of traumatic event, nightmares, intrusive dreams, flashbacks or other intense or prolonged mental distress.*

- *Having extreme arousal such as: tense feeling for no reason, having anxiety attacks, dealing with obsessive behavior patterns, unable to sleep, etc.*

- *Negative thoughts and mood or feelings which may vary from a persistent and distorted sense of blame of self or others, to estrangement from others or markedly diminished interest in all activities, an inability to remember key aspects of the event.*

Furthermore, the victim frequently experience memory lapses and cannot recall key event in their lives. I also experienced this for at least 8 years after the physical and mental abuse occurred. I found myself asking my friend about dates and years. Since I had major memory gaps missing from my memory.

PTSD Preschool Subtype and PTSD Dissociative Subtype

According to PTSD Preschool subtype they used to diagnose PTSD in children much younger than 6 years. Post-traumatic stress disorder is now refer to being developmentally sensitive, meaning that diagnostic thresholds have been lowered for children and adolescents. Next the PTSD Dissociative Subtype based upon prominent dissociative symptoms. The symptoms can be either experiences of feeling detached from one's own mind or body, or experiences in which the world seems unreal, dreamlike or distorted.

Acute Stress Disorder

Acute Stress Disorder is similar to the PTSD criteria, for consistency's sake. Currently a person cannot qualify for traumatic events whether experienced directly, witnessed, or experienced indirectly based upon the DSM IV - 5. Next, according to the DSM-IV regardless of the person reaction to the traumatic event (e.g., "the person's response involved intense fear, helplessness, or horror") has been eliminated. These criteria appeared to have little diagnostic utility.

Moreover, acute posttraumatic reactions are very heterogeneous. Heterogeneous from my perspective means that it consist of varies parts and components. Although the DSM-IV's emphasis on dissociative symptoms is overly

restrictive, individuals may meet diagnostic criteria in
DSM-5 for acute stress disorder if they exhibit any 9 of 14
listed symptoms in these categories: intrusion, negative
mood, dissociation, avoidance, and arousal (Grohol, 2013).
One must seek professional help it they feel that they are
demonstrating P.T.S.D symptoms similar to this diagnosed.

Herman's (1992) diagnosis of complex post traumatic stress disorder is as following:

1. A history of subjection to totalitarian control over a prolonged period (months to years). For example; hostages, prisoners of war, concentration camp-survivors, and survivors of some religious cults. Examples also include those subjected to totalitarian systems in sexual and domestic life, including survivors of domestic battering, childhood physical or sexual abuse, and organized sexual exploitation.
2. Alterations in affect regulations, including:
   - Persistent dysphoria,

- Chronic suicidal preoccupation,

- Self-injury,

- Explosive or extremely inhibited anger, and

- Compulsive or extremely inhibited sexuality.

3. Alterations in consciousness, including:

   - Amnesia or hypermnesia for traumatic events,

   - Transient dissociate episodes,

   - Depersonalization/derealization, and

   - Reliving experience, either in the form of intrusive post-traumatic stress disorder symptoms or in the form of ruminative preoccupation.

4. Alterations in self-perception, including:

   - Sense of helplessness or paralysis of initiative,

   - Shame, guilt, and self-blame,

   - Sense of defilement or stigma, and

   - Sense of complete difference from others.

5. Alterations in relations with others, including:

   - Isolation and withdrawal,

   - Disruption in intimate relationships,

   - Repeated search for rescuer,

- Persistent distrust, and

- Repeated failures of self-protection (Herman, 1992, p. 121).

Trauma

When a person is exposed to triggering events that resemble or symbolize an aspect of previous traumatic events it can cause a person to reexperienced the trauma. The DSM IV (1994) defines Trauma as one in which:

a.) the person experienced, witnessed or was confronted with an event that involved actual or perceived threat to life or physical integrity; and

b.) The person's emotional response to this event included horror, helplessness, or intense fear (DSM IV, 1994, pp.427-428).

During and after a traumatic experience, adaptation and new approaches that are survival-oriented for the situation are demanded. The problem comes following the trauma, when those approaches and survivalist responses are no longer functional. Recovery involves recognizing what responses are and are not functional.

As stated previously, trauma can cause changes in the brain chemistry, and changes that are helpful in short term but are harmful in the long term. Symptomatically, the person recognizes that a traumatic event has occurred it creates overwhelming fears and leaves in its wake feelings that the world is not a safe place.

Some further effects of a single-instance trauma as related to the emotional is shock, denial, confusion, disorientation, numbness, panic, weeping, extreme anxiety, insecurity, inflexibility and dissociation. Cognitive is the disbelief, disorientation and confusion, difficulty thinking, unwanted thoughts, perceptions problems, traumatic memories, and forgetfulness. Hyperarousal is when a person has trouble sleeping, trouble concentrating, heightened vigilance, easily startling, being wary, sudden tears or anger, and increased alertness. The body experience gastrointestinal symptoms, headaches, allergy symptoms, and menstrual problems (Sheahan,

Herman-Dunn; Dayton and Jaffray, 1999). The effect of prolonged repeated trauma is Posttraumatic stress disorder, complex Posttraumatic stress disorder, or medical/physical problems (Herman, 1992; Colodzin, 1993).

Furthermore, traumatic experiences are common for urban minority children, who may be at risk for a multitude of stressful life events when they live in disadvantaged, low-income neighborhoods (Attar, Guerra & Torran, 1994). In sum, the exposure and increased risks for victimization occurs frequently in adults. As will be seen later in this paper, this especially true among African American women.

Insidious Trauma

Root (1992) suggests that the concept of insidious trauma is important to understanding the experiences and cognitive schemas that determine one's subjective experiences that define a traumatic event. Insidious trauma is characterized by repetitive and cumulative experiences. It is perpetrated by persons who have power over one' access to resources and one's destiny, and directed towards persons who have a lower status on some important social variable.

The types of experiences that form insidious traumas are repeated oppression, violence, genocide, or feticide- both historical and contemporary. The effects of insidious trauma can be passed down transgenerational through stories of atrocited about what has been down to those who have come before (Hine, 1989).

Unlike many traumas, insidious traumas in context are often perceived as malicious and personal. When traumas are perceived as person-perpetualed they tend to result in negative self-evaluation and a tendency to view the world as a malevolent environment. Thus, part of the damage of this type is the difficulty in trusting others and evens self (Root, 1992).

Insidious traumas' imprinting rests on an acute self-awareness that one's safety is tentative. One comes to this conclusion by experiences that show that a fundamental, unchangeable aspect of one's identity is used to justify unequal worth and lack of protection from danger. The

result is that most women are at times acutely aware
of being female and the risk associated with it. This is
manifested in a fear of being raped, fear of walking to one's
car alone, choosing apartments off ground level, and so on.

Likewise, in order to protect themselves some women
of color are daily aware that they are not-white and
that this status is unsafe. Other persons of color may
consciously or unconsciously perform a "head count"
in certain environments to note the presence of other
persons of color to assess the safety of a situation
(Marsella, Friedman, Gerrity & Scurfield 1997).

Domestic Violence

"Domestic violence is the patterned and repeated
use of coercive and controlling behavior to limit, direct,
and shape a partner's thoughts, feelings, and actions
(Almedia, Woods, Messineo & Font, 1998). An array of
power and control tactics can be use along a continuum in
concert with one another. These tactics includes: physical
abuse, emotional abuse, economic abuse, threats and

intimidation, isolation and entrapment, sexual abuse
and exploitation, control and abuse of children, and
isolation through job relocation and language barriers.
Undocumented immigrant women are at greater risk for
abuse along the latter dimensions due to the added the
threat of deportation" (Almeida, Woods, Messineo & Font,
1998)

Domestic violence can be shaped by the structures
of domination that organize intimate partnering along
the following dimensions: emotional connection to
emotional isolation, physical affection to physical abuse,
equitable economic power to misuses and abuses of
economic power. The shared child rearing, neglect, abuse
in parenting, and sexual intimacy to sexual abuse (Almeida,
Woods, Messineo, Font, & Heer, 1994 & Renzetti, 1996)

Domestic violence affects as many as four million
women per year. For instance, seventeen million out of
the forty million are African American women who have
experienced domestic violence. Women in the United
States are more at risk for being assaulted, injured, raped,

and murdered by a current or past male partner than other types of assaisailts combined (Marsh, 1993).

African American women are more described as survivors of abuse and oppressive economic, educational, and social conditions, as well as the gatekeepers of family life (Hill, Hawkins, Rapso, & Carr, 1995). However abuse, neglect, and oppression can erode the strengths of even the most resilient woman. Violence and trauma can diminish women's opportunities to develop healthy relationships (Hill, Hawkins, Rapso, & Carr, 1995).

Wyatt, Axelrod, Chin, Carmona, and Loeb (2000) stated that domestic violence among African American women is likely with the following:

a) Child abuse, especially sexual abuse, physical abuse, and neglect will increase the likelihood of partner violence in adulthood, and b) Other traumatic events, including life-threatening or seriously distressing events, will increase women's risks for partner violence.

Fifty-six percent of women who experience any partner violence are diagnosed with a psychiatric disorder. Twenty-nine percent of all women who attempt suicide were battered, thirty seven percent of battered women have symptoms of depression, and forty-six percent have symptoms of anxiety disorder and forty–five percent experience Posttraumatic Stress Disorder (Moffit, Caspi & Silva, 1998).

Abuse

Soukhanov (1992) defined abuse as, to use wrongly or improperly, misuse, to hurt or injure a person or thing by physical or emotional maltreatment. Also, to deceive or trick a person, to revile and the use of insulting words. Kinchin (1998) focused on how abuse of any kind can affect a person; health and day to day functioning. He pointed to a wide range of feelings and emotions that a person experiences after an abuse incident.

Kinchin (1998) stated that women and men alternate between anger and fear, helplessness and vulnerability, sadness and depression, guilt and shame. They will experience feelings and thoughts around being responsible for what has happened to them. These kinds of experiences can be confusing and frustrating. Of note is the possibility that these kinds of feelings of sympathy are responsible for the tied of loyalty in cases of abuse and battering. Prolonged abuse can have a devastating effect upon the lives of the victims.

Understanding Relationships with Significant Others

Women PTSD symptoms are characterize by how it interfere with trust, emotional closeness, communication, responsible assertiveness, and effective problem solving (National Center for PTSD, 1999).

Perhaps PTSD symptoms hinder women's ability to participate in social relationships and to engage in sexual activities. The victim may also report feelings distant from others, as well as feeling emotionally numbed. Their partners, friends, or others may feel hurt, alienated, or discouraged, and then become angry or distant toward the survivor. Especially when the victim decides to move on with their life in spite of their recent abusive situation. This can be a difficult thing to do like starting a new relationship with another partner. The new partner will feel the same hurt at times of the victim. Therefore it is very important for the victim to get help as soon as possible to deal with the past.

Next, feeling irritable, on-guard, worried, or anxious may lead survivors to be unable to relax, socialize, or be intimate without being tense or demanding. In my private practice my clients has reported that their significant others feel pressured, tense, and controlled. Addition, it is difficulty falling or staying asleep and severe nightmares prevent both the survivor and partner as stated earlier in my book. As a beginning clinician in the field I have experienced so much countertransference and transference issues around my stuff. Since I had no prior education and training on how to deal with my stuff. Therefore I decided to work with my individual therapist to come up with healthy coping strategies. Fortunately for me what I found out to be helpful for me as a counselor was talking to another therapist to balance things out for myself. I usually treat the victim and abuser in separate sessions.

Another factor dealing with understanding relationship is ongoing trauma memories, trauma reminders and flashbacks. My client has also reported that living with survivor feel like living in a war zone or living in constant threat of vague but terrible danger. It is like walking on eggshell with a person who has survived domestic violence (traumatic event).

Victims often struggle with intense anger and impulses that usually are suppressed by avoiding closeness or by adopting an attitude of criticism or dissatisfaction with loved ones and friends. Since they believe if they avoid becoming serious with a potential partner they are protect from being hurt again. Intimate relationships may have episodes of verbal or physical violence.

Survivors may be overly dependent upon or overprotective of partners, family members, friends, or support persons (such as healthcare providers or therapists).
Alcohol abuse and substance addiction can be use as an attempt to cope with PTSD. This can destroy intimacy and friendships relationships (National Center for PTSD, 1999).

Understanding PTSD, Abuse, Trauma and Relationships

When women are in bad relationships, they frequently try to deny the abuse. They hope that things will change. Frequently, they might feel that nothing overtly abusive is going on in their relationships and might report that everything is well. Yet their relationship lacks life, inhibits trust, and is unfulfilling. If a female partner is unwilling to relate as a courageous, vulnerable, strong woman, perhaps it is important to question the nature of the relationship (Bass & Davis, 1994).

How Does Women Cope with Abuse, Trauma, and Posttraumatic Stress Disorder?

Some women cope with domestic violence and trauma by remaining in the relationships or fighting back. Bass and Davis (1994) stated that some survivors criticize themselves for the way they stayed in their relationship. These authors emphasized that there is no reason to be ashamed of the way women cope with the abuse and trauma. They further focused on some of the ways women cope and how it can develop into a variety of strengths (i.e., being successful at your work, becoming self-sufficient, developing a sense of humor, being good in a crisis). On the other hand, some coping mechanism become self-defeating patterns (i.e., stealing, use of drug or alcohol, or compulsive overeating).

Often one behavior will have both healthy and destructive aspects. Healing requires that the individual differentiate between the two, where a person can celebrate their strengths while changing the patterns that no longer serve their purpose.

Bass and Davis (1994) identify four ways in knowing how to change the cycle of abuse in women with PTSD. First, the definition of minimizing is a means to pretend that whatever happened wasn't that bad. Second, rationalizing is a means by which a person explains away abuse. Thirdly, denying is turning your head the older way and pretending that whatever happened did not occur. Finally, forgetting is one of the most common and effective ways people deal with trauma and abuse.

The human mind has tremendous powers of repression. The capacity to forget explains why so many trauma survivors are unaware of the fact that they were abused (Bass & Davis, 1994).

Hattendondorf, Ottens, and Lomax (1999) studied eighteen women who were assessing for frequency and severity of lifetime PTSD symptoms and the type of abuse endured. They found out that women who killed their partners have been the target of extreme violence, abuse and murderous threats for years. These women were charged with murder and were incarcerated for murdering their spouses when they decided to fight back for their lives.

Walker (1984) found that battered women who killed their partners differed from battered women who do not kill their partners; only in the amount of violence they endured. Those women who killed were subjected to greater and more frequent violence, especially of degrading sexual nature, and resulted in more serious injuries.

Torrey (1994) and Walker (1984) noted the difference between the males who were killed by their female partners and those who were not. The batterers who were killed perpetrated more frequent and severe abuse against the women. Also, expanded abuse to include another, usually a child or pet; verbalized their intentions to kill; increased their use of alcohol and drugs; and escalated the menacing nature of the violence through the brandishing of weapons.

Torrey (1994) and Walker (1991, 1999) emphasized a sense of helplessness and perception of diminishing alternatives which; dominated the psychological state of a battered woman who kills. The helplessness may stem from the fear of leaving a vindictive partner and the lack of trust in the legal system. It is to see how homicidally battered women might attempt suicide by drug overdose as a cry for help. When that kind of method fails, the women perceived that the only way to escape is to kill the batter before he kills her.

Shape and Cohen (1999) indicated that one out of twelve women strike back. The events that trigger the violence are primarily rape or other physical assaults, childhood sexual or other abuse, natural disasters, serious accidents, the sudden unexpected death of a loved one, even being diagnosed with a life –threatening illness.

Odarijew (1998) tells her story of sexual harassment and abuse while enlisted in the Canadian Air Force from 1977-1991. She stated that two of her male colleagues came to her hotel room after 11:00 p.m. in 1981. They sexual assaulted her. They were staying in a small inn and nobody was around to help her. She was a flight engineer on the Brian Mulroney's Challenger jet. She was the third person in the cockpit responsible for maintaining the aircraft systems. Upon reflection she stated that the sexual harassment start when she first joined the military in 1977.

She discussed that in 1983 when she returned from a search-rescue on Lake Ontario an incident happened on the base in Trenton. A male officer forced himself on her. Hearing about this incident caused Odarijew to reexperienced, or relive her abuse in a traumatic way. She attempted to get help from her supervisors, the base commanders, the social workers and the padres. They did not help her at the time and her experience and her PTSD went untreated. In 1994, she saw a psychiatrist who later diagnosed her with chronic post-traumatic stress disorder. She quit the military in 1997, after 20 years of service due to a medical discharge.

Religious and Cultural Issues

Religion and spirituality may serve either as mechanisms for achieving resilience in the face of domestic assault or as contributors to women's vulternability. Some religious traditions hold that even in the face of abuse, women must not separate from or divorce their partners. Furthermore, some individuals have used biblical references to legitimize the use of physical coercion as a strategy for getting women to submit to the authority of the men in their lives (Bell and Mattis, 2000).

Weems (1995) argued that biblical references to the violent control of women could be misogyny in disguise. African American women especially were Encourage to identify theologically accurate readings of partner abuse and theologically sound understandings of the sacrament of marriage.

Dake (1991) focused on how those men would not hearken to God. From his example in the Dakes Holy Bible, men continue to abuse women for their own selfish reasons. He gave an example of a man who "took his concubine, brought her forth unto men, they knew her, and abused her all night until the morning. When the day began to spring forth, they let her go. The woman in the dawning in the day and felled down at the door of the man's house; where her lord was, until it was light. Her lord up early in the morning, opened the doors of the house, and went out to go his way. Behold, the woman his concubine fallen down at the door of the house, and her hands were upon the threshold.

He said unto her, get up, and let us be going. She did not reply. Then the man took her up upon the ass and the man rose up, and gave her unto his place. When he came into his house, he took a knife, laid hold on his concubine, divides her, together with her boned, into twelve pieces, and sent her into all the coasts of Israel. There was no such deed done and seen from the day that the children of Israel came up out of the land of Egypt unto this day". He emphasizes the importance of "taking advice and speaking your minds (Dakes, 1991).

This was about a concubine in the Dakes Holy Bible who was abused all night by Sodomites' men of Gibeah. She died from the sexual abused and the cutting of her body into pieces.

Women, who come from a local church or ministry, often choose to remain in abusive marriages or relationships due to their religious beliefs. They might feel that they are disobeying God if they leave the relationship. They believe that the man is the head of the household and their role is to be submissive to the man regardless of the trauma and abuse.

A man's violence against his partner is inextricably linked to his perception of the world and his woman's place in it. Pence and Paymar (1993) emphasized the point that without a change in his world view, the violent man will continue to find "legitimate" reasons to impose his will on his partner physically.

Dake (1991) quoted that "a woman hath not power of her own body". He wanted his readers "to know that the head of every man is Christ, the head of every woman is man, and the head of Christ is God. Neither was the man created for the woman, but the woman for the man." These statements could imply to women who come from a religious background that they have no right to voice their opinions or make decisions for themselves. They need to consult with, and get their husbands approval before deciding upon anything.

As can be seen, some women's lives are about bondage, based upon their religious convictions. Dakes (1991) further point out if the" wife departs from her husband. "Let not the Christian wife divorces her husband if he be pleased to dwell with her". Ministers or priests can abuse and misuse these scriptures in relating to marriage couples who are experiencing domestic violence, abuse and traumatic events of any kind, when they urge them to stay together.

Religious leaders use the Holy Bible and other commentaries to provide counseling to marriage couples and singles to prompt them to stay in the relationships. They might encourage the person or couple to pray about seeking God's directions. They say that God is able to do anything but fail. However, the person remains unable to leave the relationship.

African American culture can be conceptualized as a complex system of symbolic forms as (e.g. folkways, mores, language, religion, gender roles, child rearing practices, rituals, metaphors, medicines and healing practices, music, and fighting behavior). They employed and socially transmitted by people of African descent who have been socialized in the United States (Bell and Mattis, 2000).

Geertz (1973) defined culture as a "historically transmitted pattern of meanings embodied in symbols, a system of inherited conceptions expressed in symbolic forms of which men communicate, perpetuate, and develop their knowledge about and attitudes toward life".

PTSD and the Legal System

Kinchin (1998) focused on the legal actions taken in dealing with Posttraumatic Stress Disorder. He stated that many physical and sexual assaults result in criminal proceeding against the assailant. He was a victim of an assault and trauma. He stated that, "a PTSD suffer is likely to be the primarily prosecution witness". The matter does not end with the dictation of a witness statement. The victims might be asking to identify the accused.

A second, or even third, statement may be needed. Eventually, a court appearance may be required. When a person appears in court they need to be carefully prepared for the court hearing by their attorney and therapist. This process can be intimidating for the PTSD victim. Even after the appearance and the legal issues, it is not over. Either side may appeal to a higher court if the outcome is not what they expected it to be. This might mean that the PTSD sufferer may have to go through the process all over again. This process could take months to years. It is easy to imagine the reason why many PTSD sufferers do not report abuse of this nature to police. It is hardly surprising that some PTSD victims have been guilty of crimes themselves. There have been instances of assault, robbery and even murder which, it is claimed, are an indirect result of suffering from PTSD (Kinchin, 1998).

Untreated victims of PTSD or even those who are fully recovered are prone to intrusive memories and sudden flashbacks of the traumatic event. Standing in a witness box, hostile crossing- examination may act as a trigger to the body's emergency mobilization systems and may cause the victim to reexerpirence the terror of the original traumatic event.

Van der Kolk and Rice-Smith (1993) stated that a person develops amnesia after a single traumatic event and may not remember the incident for years or possibly never. Their personality can split into differ personalities as well, as a way of to protecting themselves. They will go so for as to report no conscious knowledge of the abuse. They focused on how people knit their trauma together and attempt to make sense out of it at times. This is known as the fragment memory.

Women of Color and Abuse

Bell and Mattis (2000) explained their approach to domestic violence as ecophenomenological of African American culture, which is the cycle of the abuse. They hold that the violence that African American women experience in domestic sphere of life is incited, maintained, or exacerbated by an array of social-historical, institutional, community, family, and individual-level conditions and experiences. This model is grounded in the experiences of African American women.

African American women are represented as individuals who are wield and display unnatural amount of sexual, social, physical, and economic power in the domestic sphere (Jewell, 1993; Roberts, 1997). Some of the stereotypes of African American women are that they are dark complexioned, mentally ill, overweight, verbally assertive, and just fight back. They are perceived as "inauthentic victims" (Bell & Mattis, 2000).

Richie (1996) pointed out that African American women who are victims of domestic violence often adhere quite strictly to the values of mainstream culture. Their responses and feelings about cultural norms are extreme and inflexible. They still desire a nuclear family despite the personal cost and abuse issues. He stated "that loyalty is at the root of their vulnerability within their relationships" (Richie, 1996).

He explained how African Americans' women identities are centered on pleasing others and holding privileged positions in their families of origin. They are expected to achieve and maintained their privileged status. Also, they end to believe in the importance of the perfect nuclear family, believe in the ideology of the African American male as a victimizer and accept that there is a need for African American women to protect the men at all costs (Richie, 1996).

Many of the traumas affecting women are common, repeated, and current. These traumas include contextual threats through the interplay of domination by gender or race or ethnicity that threaten safety, limit the mobility, and denigrate the self-worth of an individual by virtue of a status she is born into.

Even the notion of "post"- trauma responding largely originates in the White male experience of time-limited events, often singular in nature versus the prolonged, everyday effects of rape, and sexual and physical assault (Marsella, Friedman, Gerrity & Scurfield, 1997).

Childhood Maltreatment and Suicidal Behavior among African American Women

Childhood maltreatment and suicidal behavior among African American women shows how PTSD and suicidal behavior might be related to childhood abuse. Thompson, Kaslow, Lane & Kingree (2000) studied 335 African American Women to explore their history of attempted suicide due to childhood sexual, physical or emotional abuse and current PTSD issues. The researchers learned from this project that women with a history of childhood maltreatment are at increased risk for developing PTSD. Second, women with a history of childhood maltreatment are at increased risk for suicidal behavior. Thirdly, individuals with symptoms of PTSD are at increased risk for suicidal behaviors.

The researchers tested whether the combinations of current PTSD with a history of childhood maltreatment increased the risk for making a suicide attempt beyond that attributed to PTSD or childhood maltreatment alone. It was hypothesized that suicide attempts would evidence higher rates of all forms of childhood maltreatment and higher rates of current PTSD than their counterparts who had never made a suicide attempt.

Therefore it predicted that women with both current PTSD and a lifetime history of child maltreatment would be at greater risk for making suicide attempt than women without PTSD and no history of maltreatment (Thompson, Kaslow, Lane and Kingree, 2000).

Women with current PTSD; no history of maltreatment, and women without PTSD a history of child maltreatment. They would be at greater risk for suicidal behavior than women with neither PTSD nor a history of maltreatment. They would but less risk for suicidal behavior than women

with PTSD would and a history of child maltreatment
would.

Women with both a history of childhood sexual abuse
and current PTSD are approximately six times more likely
than women with neither PTSD nor a history of sexual
abuse to have made a nonfatal suicide attempt. Women
with PTSD but no history of childhood sexual abuse were
three times as likely as women with neither PTSD nor a
history of sexual abuse to have made a nonfatal suicide
attempt. However, child sexual abuse without concurrent
PTSD did not increase a woman's risk for suicidal behavior.

Transference and Countertransfence Issues

Corey (1996) definition of transference is when the
client's unconscious shifting to the therapist of feelings
and fantasies, both positive and negative, that are
displacements from reactions to significant others from the
client's past. The transference issues in dealing with African
American women and other nationalities are unequal in
their levels of comfort in discussing their personal problems

with a friend or therapist. An African American woman might feel that the therapist is a close friend or family member especially if the therapist is an African American. They might put all of their trust and confident in their therapist to help them deal with an abusive and traumatize relationship. They might believe that their therapist have all of the answers.

The dominant race or culture might see a therapist or medical doctor for problems for relationship problems instead of telling a close friend or a church member. The dominant race expects for the therapist or psychiatrist to have all of the answers or to give them the recipe to fixing their problems.

Corey (1996) definition of countertransference is when a therapist's unconscious emotional responses to a client that are likely to interfere with objectivity and unresolved conflicts of the therapist that are projected onto the clients. The countertransference issues in working with or dealing with women with abuses, domestic violence or PTSD issues can be difficult for a therapist who has also in a traumatized relationship. Therapists have to be careful to not allow his or her feelings to come up and to dictate the way the therapy should go for their clients.

Limitations and Challenges

The primary limitation and challenge in examining the issues of relationships with African American women with PTSD is the lack of empirical evidence available. Some of the anecdotal statements and status quote from society. Some of the stereotypes statements that society makes about women's role are that they are their relationship are to be subject to their spouses or their significant others (i.e., obedience and practice loyalty in their relationships). It was extremely difficult to clarify how women function, maintain control of their lives and to gather information on minorities.

Thus, in writing this paper, I focused on exploring or examining the definitions, symptoms of PTSD and to gradually to focus on women relationships. However, I was able to find some research articles and books on women that have been diagnosed with PTSD this was helpful. These was not enough information on other minorities since the majority of the information on PTSD and relationships or domestic violence issues was reported as being about the same for all women.

Discussion

I believed that some cultures condone domestic violence and abuse. I am an African American female who comes from a traditional Bible belt setting. I was born and reared in the State of Mississippi for most of my life. From the age of three to twenty eight years old, I witnessed African American men physically, emotionally, and sexually abusing, and traumatizing their partners. I assumed earlier in life that it was O.K. on some level for a man to abuse a woman, since; the women never left their relationships.

I wondered why they stayed and did not seek for help. I believed that these women felt like they had no way out. The women in my old neighborhood had anywhere from four children to nineteen children. They said they remained in their relationships so they could provide shelter and food for their children. My mother lived in an abusive relationship for twenty years.

It was brought to my attention by a friend of mine that my mother told a friend of mine that she was not happy in her marriage with my father for the first ten years. She said she took all of the beatings and cheating, and isolation so she could provide for us. It took some years before the abuse stopped, time for her to learn how to forgive and to love him again. She stated that the abused stopped after twenty years of marriage"; they were married for thirty years. This was a shocking revelation for me. Then, I realized from my mother's story that most of the women in my neighborhood were unhappy and abused by their partners.

Orhberg (1999) stated that victims stay in relationships because they feel that there is no way out, they have no resources, they are of the legal system, they are ashamed, and difficulty in assessing the welfare department. Women might be afraid of Child Protective Service taking their children away due to domestic violence reports and arrests. Therefore, women decide to stay in abusive relationships for various reasons. This author discussed the fact that these women love was base upon aberrant attraction to a sadistic sexual partner.

Donnelly, Cook, and Wilson (1999) explored the services that are available in three southern states for battered women or abused women. The southern states were Alabama, Georgia, and Mississippi. The researchers learned that women of color, lesbians, middle-class women, rural women, the homeless, the mentally ill, and the elderly women were viewed in stereotypical ways. They reported that in these states it is hard for women of colors to receive services immediately or first. These states mainly serve the dominant race immediately. Therefore, women of colors sometime do not report the incident. The State of Mississippi received about $27, 000.00 per year, Georgia state receive $21, 000.00 and the state of Alabama receive about $80, 769.00 per year to run the battered women shelters.

The researchers in this journal article were given a range of explanations on why women of color did not receive the same kinds of services as the dominant race. For example, the agencies stated that people of color have their own shelters and support groups, which is do include mental treatment. They are even excluded due to pressure from outsiders.

Survival and Transformation

The road to survival and recovery included developing a coping pan. This has not been an easy process for me. This plan consisted of using my natural support system (family and friends), utilizing my church family, attending the Women in Transition classes, and going to relationship counseling session. It was not until I located to Washington State that my life was transformed into something beautiful. It is like I had a second chance to improve and reinvent. Read Below how I transformed from being a victim to not being a victim.

I have committed myself to public service throughout my career and am a firm believer in supporting city government. Examples of my experience includes:

- <u>Volunteerism Experience (current):</u> Washington State School Counselors Association as a committee member of the Guidance and Counseling State Task force group with the Office of Superintendent Public Instruction and on the Ethics Board for Washington State School counselors. Secretary and treasurer for Bremerton Ministerial Alliance Organization

- <u>Political Experience:</u> Elected to Office by the citizens of the City of Bremerton for two conservative terms as a School Board Director My previous experienced as an elected official of the Bremerton School board qualifies me as a Bremerton City Council member. My responsibility encompassed overseeing the capital and general funds budget, setting budget priorities, hiring employees, hiring chief executive officer, and implementing school board policies. Positions held as a Bremerton School District Director included President, Vice President, and a Judge for the Washington School Board Directors' Diversity Committee.

- Professional Experience: Current Guidance Counselor at Washington Youth Academy, 25 years Plus in mental health and social service field Supervised State Chemical Dependency Unit in Mississippi Vocational Rehabilitation Counselor in District of Columbia Sociology Instructor in the District of Columbia

- Additional Board on Appointments: Served on Kitsap Mental Health Executive Board of Directors in 2009 -2012. Vice President of the Pacific Northwest Women Auxiliaries for 3 years which consisted of State of Washington, Canada, Akaka, and Oregon.

- Published Author: How Does Posttraumatic Stress Disorder Affect the Intimate Relationships of Women of Color? (1st Edition) 2000

<u>Business Owner:</u> Galloway counseling and Referral Services 1997 to 2007 in the Downtown Bremerton area.

- <u>Currently</u> enrolled in college and working with local ministries within Washington State.

Summary and Conclusion

This research book focused on terminology and explored the DSM IV criteria of PTSD and Trauma. PTSD diagnoses were initially given to Vietnam veterans and Prisoners of war first. Later, the psychologists and therapists began to use the PTSD diagnosis with the public. PTSD can be defined as an extreme stressors involving direct personal experience of an event that involves actual or threatened death or serious injury. Other threats will include those to one's integrity or the witnessing an event that involves death, injury, and threat to physical integrity of another person, (e.g., when learning of an unexpected or violent death, serious harm; or threat of death or injury experienced by a family member or close associate).

Domestic violence and abuse is when a person is controlled by another individual sexually, physically or emotionally. This book pointed out, that repeated use of coercion and power can result in PTSD symptoms.

Women's relationships with significant others can be traumatic, paralyzing, and abusive. As stated earlier in this book, women with PTSD typically do not report feeling close to their partner, having difficulty communicating, show a loss of interest in sexual or social activities, feel numb, distance themselves from their partner. These women also reported that they experience have flashbacks, reliving the traumatic events, and have difficult falling asleep at night. Women who are abuse by their partners often minimize the abuse and trauma. They want to be seen as a strong person in life.

Women cope with abuse, trauma and PTSD diagnosis in various ways. Some of the ways are:

- they fail to speak up,
- fail to seek for help
- other women seek help from local churches and friends,
- other killed their partners,
- Some women attempt to sexually or physically please their partners, rationalizing, denying, and trying not to think about the abuse.

When, women fight back they could end up in the prison system. I do not believe that this is right when women have been traumatize and abused by their partners for years. Especially, when the victims called the police department, women's shelters, and the sexual assault centers and received insufficient help. This can be discouraging process for the victims and significant others. The alarming fact about this process is that women could be incarcerated and receives limited services while serving time in prison. I believe that women who have been incarnate in prison need to see a counselor and psychiatrist for these types of crimes regularly.

Religious, legal and cultural factors continue to influence the way women understand and deal with domestic violence, abuse and PTSD issues. Some religious organization uses the Holy Bible as a means to control or insist on couples staying together regardless of the circumstances. The biblical scriptures they use come from the King James Versions and other Biblical versions. These are some of the scriptures use in religious counseling I

Corinthians 7:4, I Corinthians 7:10, I Corinthians 11:3, 9 and I Corinthians 13:16.

When victims go to court or report an incident of abuse this could lead to a traumatic experience; or even cause the person to relive the original situation. The investigation process itself can be a nightmare for the victims. Some victims do not recall the abuse or traumatic events for years, or never remember the entire event in detail.

African American women unique issues are related to their family of origins, belief system, religious orientation, and economical status. I believed that women of color have experience physical and sexual abuse for over 100 years. African American women might feel inferior to the dominant race; therefore, they might not seek for help from traditional organizations.

They might believe that the mainstream society thinks that they are low class citizens or just stupid people. African American women are extremely loyal and depend upon their partner mainly due to traditions. Some, African

American women do not leave abusive relationships since they feel that this would mean that they are a failure.

Other minorities women have accept the fact that their partners could be abusive on an on going basis. They continue to allow their partners to violate them. They appear to be powerless over their situations. They feel that they need to remain in their relationships since they want to be a good wife. When women have a prior history of being sexually and physically abused as children they tend to be at a greater risk of domestic violence and having PTSD symptoms. They are at a higher risk for suicidal ideation and making suicidal attempts.

Further research might explore the beginning clinician's experiences around countertransference issues. It might be that if the clinician has a past history of being abused, depressed, and traumatized around domestic violence issues. For example, the clinician might attempt to work with her stuff in sessions or just get stuck in treatment with a client based upon where she is in her own treatment.

This type of dynamic might cause a clinician to relive or reexperienced her own trauma again if she has not done her own work. I believe that a clinician need to be aware of her biases, weakness, and strengths in order to provide quality services to this population. It is difficult at times to know how a client feel in treatment. A client might experience transference issues in therapy. For example, a client might see the clinician as a family member, spouse or friend this could cause all kinds of verbal and nonverbal responses to treatment. He or she might believe that the clinician has all of the answers to their problems or have difficulty with trust. Women can only respond to treatment based on their belief systems and abusive histories.

The purpose of this research book is to increase the level of sensitivity to women of color who are dealing with domestic violence and PTSD issues. Beyond exploring this population more closely, it would be helpful for women's shelters to do a more thorough assessment of the clients' family of origin, criminal arrest record, and spousal abuse history. Women shelters need to have a doctor and counselors onsite to debrief women and to refer them out to mental health centers for supportive counseling.

Finally, there is a need for women shelters' directors, psychologists, and therapists to write grant proposals for additional services to help women in time of crises. It is also prudent for clinicians to go to seminars and conferences to stay abreast of changes and services that are available for this population. Also to subscribe to professional journals and purchase books related to women issues would be helpful.

Comments and feedback

Submit to: Galloway.c.t.95@gmail.com

References

Almeida, R., Woods, R., Messineo, T. & Font, R. (1988). Cultural context model. In McGoldrick (Ed.), Re-visioning family therapy. Race, culture, and gender in clinical practice (pp. 404-432) New York: Guilford.

Almeida, R., Woods, R., Messineo, T., Font, R., & Heer, C. (1994). Violence in the lives of the racially and sexually different. A public and private dilemma. In R. Almeida (Ed.) Experiences of feminist family therapy through diversity (pp. 99-126). New York: Harrington Park.

American Psychiatric Association (2013). Diagnostic and statistical manual of mental disorders. (5th ed.). Washington, DC: Author

American Psychiatric Association. (1980). Diagnostic and statistical manual of mental disorders. (3rd ed.) Washington, DC: Author.

American Psychiatric Association (1994). Diagnostic and statistical manual of mental disorders. (4th ed.). (pp. 424-427). Washington, DC: Author

Attar, Guerra & Torran (1994). Neighborhood disadvantage, stressful life events, and adjustments in urban elementary-school children. Journal of Clinical Child Psychology, 23, 391- 400.

Bass, E. & Davis, L. (1994). The courage to heal: A guide for women survivor. (pp. 44-46, 47, 244-248). New York, Harper Collins.

Bell, C. & Mattis, J. (2000). The importance of cultural competence in ministering to African American victims of domestic violence. Violence Against Women. (Vol. 6. pp. 515-532). Thousand Oaks, California. Sage Publication.

Bogdanos, M. (2013). Signs of Emotional Abuse. Psych Central. http://psychcentral.com/blog/archives/2013/02/20/signs-of-emotional-abuse

Colodzin, B. (1993). How to survive trauma. Barrytown, New York: Station Hill Press.

Corey, G. (1996) Theory and practice of counseling and psychotherapy. (5th ed.) (pp.86-87). Pacific Grove, CA Brooks/Cole Publishing Company.

Dake, F. (1991). Dakes's annotated reference bible. The Holy Bible. Old and New testaments. In King James Version. (pp. 180,183-186, 286-287). Lawrenceville, Georgia: Dake Bible Sales, INC.

Donnelly, D., Cook, K. & Wilson, L. (1999). The dual face of services to battered women in three Deep South states. Violence Against Women. (vol. 5, 710-741)Thousand Oaks, California. Sage Publications.

Geertz, C. (1973). The interpretions of cultures. New York: Basic Books.

Griffith, D & Goodwin, C (2013) Conflict Survival Kit: tools for resolving conflict at work. (2nd Ed). Pearson. New York.

Grohol, J. (2013). DSM-5 Changes: PTSD, Trauma & Stress-Related Disorders. *Psych Central*. From http://pro. psychcentral.com/2013/dsm-5-changes-ptsd-trauma-stress-related-disorders/004406.html

Hattendorf, J; Ottens, A; & Lomax, R. (1999) Type of abuse and posttraumatic stress disorder symptoms reported by women who killed abusive partners. Violence Against Women. (Vol. 5, 292-312). Thousand Oak, California. Sage Publications.

Herman, J.L. (1992) Trauma, and Recovery: The aftermath of violence—from domestic abuse to political terror. New York: Basic Books.

Hill, H.; Hawkins, SR; Rapso, M., & Carr, P. (1995). Relationship between multiple exposures to violence and coping strategies among African American mothers. Violence and Victims, 10, 55-71.

Hine, D.C. (1989) Rape and the inner lives of Black women in the Middle West: Preliminary thoughts on the culture of dissemblance. Signs, 14, 912-920.

Jewell, K. (1993). From the mammy to Ms. America and beyond: Cultural images and the shaping of U.S. policy. New York: Routledge Press.

Kinchin, D. (1998). Posttraumatic stress disorder. The invisible injury. (pp. 91-155, 155-162) Great Britain by Wessex Press, Wintage, Oxfordshire.

Marsella, A; Friedman, M; Gerrity, E. & Scurfield, R. (1997). Ethnocultural aspects of posttraumatic stress disorder. Issues, research, and clinical applications. (pp. 370-388). Washington, DC: American Psychological Association.

Marsh, C. E. (1993). Sexual assault and domestic violence in the African American community. Western Journal of Black Studies, 17(3), 149-155.

Moffit, K; Caspi, A. & Slva, P. (1998). "Comorbidity between abuse of an adult and DSM III-R Mental disorders: evidence from an epidemiological study." Washington, DC. American Journal of Psychiatry, Vol. 155 (1).

National Center for Posttraumatic Stress Disorder. (2000) PTSD and Relationships. How does trauma affect relationships? http://www.ncptsd.org./tacts/spectitic/ts-relastionships.html.

Odarijew, N (1998). <u>They ruined my life. rape.</u> (pp. 18). Maclean Hunter Consumer Publications.

Orchberg, F; MD (1999). <u>Gift from within</u>. Canden, Maine.

Pence, E. & Paymar, M. (1993) <u>Education groups for men who batter</u>. The <u>Duluth model</u>. (pp. 71). Springer Publishing Company.

Renzetti, C. (1996). The poverty of services for battered lesbians. <u>Journal of Gay and Lesbian Social Services, 4,</u> 61-68.

Richie, B. (1996). <u>Compelled crime: the gender of Black battered women.</u> New York: Routledge.

Roberts, D. (1997) <u>Killing the black body: race, reproduction and the meaning of liberty.</u> New York: Vintage Books.

Rosenbloom, D, Williams, M.B. and Watkins, B.E. (2010) Life after Trauma. (2nd ed.) A Workbook for Healing. Published by Guilford.

Root, M.P.P. (1992) Reconstructing the impact of trauma on personality. In LS Brown & M. Ballou (Eds.) Personality and psychopathology (pp. 229-265). New York: Guilford.

Shape, J.W. & Cohen, S. (1999). Posttraumatic stress disorder. Shattered. (pp. 24-29). Weider Publications.

Sheahan, G.; Herman-Dunn; Jaffray and Dayton, S (1999). Trauma/PTSD. Self-Injury. Chicago, Illinois. University of Chicago.

Soukhanov, A. (1992). The American heritage dictionary of English: language. (3rd ed.) Boston, New York. Houghton Mifflin Company.

Thompson, M., Kaslow, N., Lane, D. B. & Kingstree. (2000). Childhood maltreatment, PTSD and Suicidal behavior among African American females. Journal of Interpretation Violence. pp. 3-15 Beverly Hills

Torrey, M. (1994,) The fighting for women who fight back. The Illinois clemency projected for battered women. DePaul Law Magazine, 8-11. Trafford, A. (1991) Why battered women kill? Self defense, not revenge is often the motive. The Washington Post, p. 2 Walker, L. E. (1989). Terrifying Love. New York; Harper Row. Walker, L.E. (1991). Post-traumatic Stress disorder in women: Diagnosis and treatment of battered women syndrome. Psychotherapy, 28, 21-29. Walker, L.E.A. (1984a). The battered women syndrome. New York: Springer. Walker, L.E.A. (1984b). Psychology and violence against women. American Psychologist, 44, 695-702.

Van der Kolk, B A. & Rice-Smith, E., MD (1993). Trauma and Memory I dissociate defense Video. Cavalcade Productions.

Walker, L. (1984). The battered woman syndrome. New York: Springer.

Walker, L. (1999). Psychology and domestic violence around the world. American Psychologist, 54, 21-29. New York: Springer.

Wallace, M. (1990). Black macho and the myth of the superwoman. New York: Verso Press. In Weems, R. (1995).

Battered love: Marriage, sex, and violence in the Hebrew prophets. Minneapolis: Fortress Press.

Wyatt, G., Axelrod, J; Chin, D; Carmona, J.V. & Loeb, T. (2000). Examining patterns of vulternability to domestic violence among African American women. Violence Against Women. (Vol. 6, 495-514). Thousand Oaks: Sage Publications.

I would like to thank my Emmanuel Apostolic Church Family in Bremerton, WA for all of their support down through the years.